`When I See the Blood

Tracy Henderson

Published by Tracy Henderson, 2023.

`WHEN I SEE THE BLOOD

First edition. February 14, 2023.

Copyright © 2023 Tracy Henderson.

ISBN: 979-8215479476

Written by Tracy Henderson.

Table of Contents

I would like to dedicate this book to my family. They are very supportive and patient weith me as i write books. Without their support this could not be possible. I would also like to dedicate it to my Lord Jesus. He enables me to write. Words are just words until he takes the helm. The words then become life changing. Thank you Lord

INTRODUCTION

I was raised in church my whole life. One of my fondest memories was sitting in Sunday School class and listening to the teacher teach about all the bible characters. We learned about Adam and Eve, Samson, David, and the most important person of all, Jesus. Those days helped shape who I am today.

As I got older and started preaching, God began to build on the foundation my teacher laid in Sunday School. We talk about teachable moments all the time. As I started ministering the word, those teachable moments became more into play. There are moments so teachable as when I read the last few chapters of Genesis and the book of Exodus.

I was assigned a ten-page research paper in my English at Christian Leaders Institute. I decided to write about the Passover. This book is from the research paper. We will go in-depth and see what we can uncover. My goal is for us to capture the essence of Passover. What did the blood on the doorpost and lentil represent? Where else in the bible did this concept become important? Is there still power in the blood today?

We know the blood of Jesus is a controversial subject. It is so controversial people have wanted to take the mention of the blood out of our hymnals. I pray you will see the importance of the blood when you are done reading this book.

God told Moses to tell the children of Israel to put the blood on the doorposts and lentils of their house. He said, When I see the blood, I will pass over you. So settle into your favorite reading spot. Grab your bible and come on a journey with me back in time. Watch the preparation all the way back to Abraham. God is still calling, still mandating the blood. Can you hear him say these words in your spirit When I see the blood?

CHAPTER 1
THE BEGINNING

We read the all-familiar story in Genesis about the fall of man. Genesis 3 sets the stage for sin entering into the world. Genesis 3:1 in the NIV says; *Now the serpent was more crafty than any of the wild animals the Lord God had made. He said to the woman, "Did God really say, "You must not eat from any tree in the garden'?"*

We must understand Satan does not deal in the truth. He only tells the partial truth. In fact, God said, *"You are free to eat from any tree in the garden, but you must not eat from the tree of the knowledge of good and evil, for when you eat from it, you will certainly die."* Genesis 2:16-17.

God forbid them from eating the fruit of one tree, not every tree. We would not fall for his propaganda if Satan were to show his actual hand. He only shows you the good side. No one wants the bad, only the good. Satan knows once we see the whole picture, we will not hear anything he has to say. So, he told Eve a partial truth. God said she was not to partake of one tree, not all of them. The woman knew this to be a partial truth.

The woman said to the serpent, "We may eat fruit from the trees of the garden, but God did say, you must not eat fruit from the tree that is in the middle of the garden, and you must not touch it, or you will die" Genesis 3:2. Why do you suppose the forbidden tree was in the middle of the garden? I believe the placement of the tree in the garden was strategic. Let me explain. When Jesus was crucified, he was in the middle of two thieves. The tree in the middle of the garden represents the cross. Amazing!! It was not until I looked at what Eve told the serpent that this came to me. Touching the tree meant touching the cross. I believe Satan knew this.

"You will not certainly die," the serpent told the woman. "For God knows that when you eat from it your eyes will be opened, and you will be like God, knowing good and evil" Genesis 3:4-5. Satan tipped his hand to the woman, what he tried to accomplish when he fell. He wanted to take the place of God and was kicked out of Heaven. By the woman partaking in the forbidden tree, she was kicked out of the garden.

We read in Genesis 3 that Eve partook of the tree and gave it to Adam; he ate from it too. The minute the man ate of the tree, sin entered the world. Why? Ephesians 5:23 says *For the husband is the head of the wife, even as Christ is the head of the church: and he is the savior of the body.* So when Adam sinned, he broke rank with God. He got out of his place as the headship of his family.

Men, we must realize our place. Adam lost his place because he got out of place. God is about an order. If you don't believe that, look at the garden's placement. All the trees they could partake of were placed within reach. The tree of knowledge of good and evil was placed in the middle of the garden. The cross of Jesus, where our redemption was bought and paid for, was right in the middle of two thieves. That is order. When Adam fell, the order was disrupted. When we, as the head of our family, break rank and allow someone else to take over the headship, we also disrupt the order.

Disorder equaled broken fellowship. When Adam partook of the fruit, his eyes were opened. He realized his error. Was his error in eating? I believe his error was in breaking the fellowship with his maker. We must remember God breathed life into Adam. The first face Adam saw was God's face. When he sinned and the fellowship was broken, we could no longer see the face of God until the time of Moses. When Adam broke his fellowship with God, he had to leave the garden. Death was introduced into the world by the sin of one person, Adam's head of the family.

THE NEW BEGINNING

Some events signified how far sin had taken over the world from the time Adam sinned. Adam was a king. He had dominion over the garden. When he fell, he lost the crown. Satan took over the crown. How strategic was Satan? His goal in Heaven was to rule, and he failed. To establish a kingdom, it had to be on earth. He did that through deception. His kingdom, however, is not an everlasting kingdom. It will be stripped from him in the end.

The new beginning started with Abraham. Abraham was asked by God to leave everything he knew behind, and he would make him the father of many nations. God asks us to do the same. Abraham didn't question God but did what he asked. Abraham loved God more than anything.

We used to sing a song in church that goes like this; More than ever before, Lord, I love you. More than ever before, Lord, I need you. More than ever before, I've got to tell you. I love you now more than ever before. Do we really know what we are singing? More than life. More than family. More than wealth or anything else. Do we genuinely love the Lord with everything in us? Abraham did. How far did his love go? He gave up **EVERYTHING!!** For God. What have we given up for Christ?

Someone else gave up everything.

"For God so loved the world, that he gave his only begotten son; that whosoever believeth in him, shall not perish, but have everlasting life" John 3:16. It is my opinion Abraham giving up everything symbolizes God giving up his son Jesus for us.

He left his father and sojourned to a land he did not know. When God asked Abraham to go, he did not question him. He could have asked God what he was thinking, but he didn't. He went. What a testimony. I want that kind of testimony. Don't you?

How much did God love Abraham? He loved him so much that God told Abraham what he would do with Sodom and Gomorrah before he did it. Armed with this information, Abraham bargained with God. Because of Abraham's persistence and God's love for Abraham, Lit and his daughters were spared from the destruction of Sodom and Gomorrah. Lot's sons-in-law could have been spared, but they refused to leave. Lot's wife could have been spared, but in the midst of her leaving, she looked back and became a pillar of salt.

Satan wants us to look back to what used to be. If he can draw our attention to what will be or could be and get us to look back at what used to be, he can destroy us. Churches are full of people that looked back. I want to look forward to what God is going to do.

God put Abraham to the test. He asked Abraham to sacrifice his only son Isaac. One could argue Abraham had another son, and Isaac wasn't his only son. Let me explain this. Ishmael was what I consider his doubt son. When the angel told Abraham Sarah was going to conceive, she doubted. Sarah was well past child-bearing age, so she gave her handmaid to Abraham. Her handmaid conceived and had Ishmael. Ishmael was not the son of the promise God was talking about. When Sarah conceived, she bore the promised son, and his name was Isaac.

When God asked Abraham to give up the son of promise, Abraham did it without question. I could not do that. I lost my firstborn when I was twenty years old. I felt rejected by God and felt I was handed a raw deal. Abraham did not even consider that.

Genesis tells us Abraham and Isaac went up to the mountain. They had the wood. They had the fire, but where was the sacrifice? I can picture Abraham wrestling within himself all the way up the mountain. He trusted God, but there had to be something inside of him that questioned if he was hearing right. Have you been there? We know God spoke to us, but did we really hear correctly?

As Abraham put Isaac on the altar and had the knife ready to plunge into him, an angel stopped him. The angel drew Abraham's attention to a ram caught in the thicket. This ram represents Jesus, our substitute. We could never pay the debt we owe for our sins. The price was too steep. Jesus became Isaac so we wouldn't have to. When God looked at Isaac remembered the covenant he made with Abraham. This excites me.

The blood of the Passover symbolizes God's son. The blood of Yeshua serves as an atonement. God remembers the Messiah's sacrifice when he sees the lamb's blood.

The last chapters of Genesis set the stage for the book of Exodus. Joseph, Isaac's grandson, is sold into slavery to the Egyptians. His brothers were jealous of him because he was his father Jacob's or appropriately named Israel's favorite son.

Jacob gave Joseph a coat of many colors. Joseph had a dream that his brothers were going to bow to him. If you were one of his brothers, how would you feel when he told you that? They were angry. The dreams didn't stop there. He also dreamed his father and mother would bow to him. Wow!! That's far out. As Charles Swindow says in his book on Joseph I am reading, some people, including his brothers, would have taken this as arrogance. "Dad, I have some news to tell you. You and my brothers are going to bow to me. I don't know when, but you are." That was what he was saying to them.

Jealousy will kill you. Let's see what the Song of Solomon says in the NIV about jealousy; *Place me like a seal over your heart, like a seal on your arm; for love is as strong as death, its jealousy unyielding as the grave. It burns like a blazing fire, like a mighty flame* Song of Solomon 8:6.

Many people are getting stung by the stinger of jealousy. Churches have split because someone got jealous. Song of Solomon says jealousy is as cruel as the grave. Have you ever been victimized by someone jealous of you? The pastor goes to a higher level in God than someone thinks he should, and they get jealous. What happens when jealousy grips the heart of someone? They begin to seek revenge. Joseph's brothers wanted revenge.

His brothers had gone to graze their father's flocks near Shechem, and Israel said to Joseph, "As you know, your brothers are grazing the flocks near Shechem. Come, I am going to send you to them." "Very well," he replied.

So he said to him, "Go and see if all is well with your brothers and the flocks, and bring back word to me." Then he sent him to the Valley of Hebron. Let's drop down a few verses.

So Joseph went after his brothers and found them near Dothan. But they saw him in the distance, and they plotted to kill him before he reached them. Genesis 37:12-14, 17-18. The rest of the story tells how they stripped him of his coat and threw him into a pit. They put blood on his coat and told his father he was killed by an animal. Jealousy will not only kill but will cause you to lie as well.

Another person in the Old Testament allowed jealousy to consume them. David had slain Goliath. No one in Israel, including King Saul, could stand up to Goliath. Armed with God's spirit, David not only stood up to him but killed him. The people sang a song Saul slew his thousands but David his ten thousand. What happened? Saul got jealous and wanted David killed. Jealousy will not celebrate your achievements. Jealousy will act normal to you and slay you when you are not around. God help us to not be jealous.

God shows favor to Joseph in the land of Egypt. The favor on Joseph's life is prevalent when he is thrown into prison because he was lied to by Potiphar's wife. She claimed Joseph tried to take advantage of her and even had a piece of his clothing to back up her claims. Did Joseph give up? No, he did not. Favor went with him into Egypt and followed him into the dungeon. Glory!!

God will show you favor even amid captivity. The world expects you to fall, but God. I see this in my own life. We have been going through a situation in our family for over two years. Satan whispers in my ear "You may as well give up." The more he whispers the more favor we receive. Our enemies give us money. I'm serious. Hear what I'm saying. When God is backing you up Hell cannot stop you. When God is backing you up Hell pays the price. God was backing Joseph up in the prison.

The story winds up with Joseph getting a promotion. Did you hear that? He got a promotion. I was praying the other morning and I heard the spirit of the Lord say;" As I brought Joseph out I will bring you out. Shave yourself and change your clothes because you are coming out." I declare this year, not the calendar year, but the advent calendar, God is bringing his people out. Rosh Hashana has passed and it is a new year.

With God, a new year means a new victory. You are fixing to go to a new level. The level in God you are going not everyone is going to be able to hang with you. Fear not, God has prepared you to go to the king's house. You are going to pray differently. Before, you bound things and loosed things. Kings do this because a king is a man of war. You are going to an imperial level. You will know when to bind and when to speak imperially. I mentioned this in my last book. You will find yourself speaking what you want to take place in your life, and it will happen. OOOOOO. Take it in the spirit now as you are reading this.

When Joseph came out of the prison he shaved himself and changed his clothes. This goes deeper than we read into it. Not only did his appearance change, but his speech changed as well. It had to. He was promoted to second in command.

You are being promoted in the spirit to second in command. When Jesus changed Peter's name from Peter to the rock he changed the way he prayed. Whatever you bind on earth (kingdom) will be bound in heaven. Whatever you loose on earth (imperial) will be loosed in heaven. Glory!! Imperial speech commands things to happen. You can speak a new car into your driveway. I know you are saying another name it claim it preacher. Listen.

I worked at Pepsi. I had to work every Sunday and I wanted to be in church. One day a boldness rose up in me. I went around at work saying "This is my last Sunday stocking soda at Wal-Mart." I walked up to co- workers and told them this was my last Sunday. Two days later I got a call from Walgreens (where I work now). My schedule is Mon, Tuesday, Wednesday 5:30 A.M. To 3:30 P.M. Off Thursday. Work Friday and off Saturday and Sunday. I was hired as a temp. Two weeks after I started the boss in the shipping department came up to me and told me he would help me get hired on. Last month I was hired on. I kept my schedule but changed positions. I'm telling you God will change the way you pray in this level.

Joseph was not only reunited with his family, but his family bowed to him just like he dreamed. Whatever God has shown you take it top the bank because it will happen as he shows it to you. Hallelujah!!!

And he gave him the covenant of circumcision: and so Abraham begat Isaac, and circumcised him the eighth day; and Isaac begat Jacob; and Jacob begat the twelve patriarchs.

And the patriarchs, moved with envy, sold Joseph into Egypt: but God was with him,

And delivered him out of all his afflictions, and gave him favour and wisdom in the sight of Pharaoh king of Egypt; and he made him governor over Egypt and all his house.

Now there came a dearth over all the land of Egypt and Chanaan, and great affliction: and our fathers found no sustenance.

But when Jacob heard that there was corn in Egypt, he sent out our fathers first.

And at the second time Joseph was made known to his brethren; and Joseph's kindred was made known unto Pharaoh.

Then sent Joseph, and called his father Jacob to him, and all his kindred, threescore and fifteen souls.

So Jacob went down into Egypt, and died, he, and our fathers,

And were carried over into Sychem, and laid in the sepulchre that Abraham bought for a sum of money of the sons of Emmor the father of Sychem.

But when the time of the promise drew nigh, which God had sworn to Abraham, the people grew and multiplied in Egypt,

Till another king arose, which knew not Joseph.

The same dealt subtilly with our kindred, and evil entreated our fathers, so that they cast out their young children, to the end they might not live. Acts 7:8-19.

Chapter 2
MOSES

" M *oses may have seemed an unlikely choice, but the Lord knew how to make him a great leader" Charles Stanley.*

God has a way of taking the unlikely and making it the likely. Such was the case with Moses. Moses did not start out as a great leader. Let's go back to Acts 7 and see what Stephen had to say about the account of Moses. What can be gleaned from what Stephen says?

In which time Moses was born, and was exceeding fair, and nourished up in his father's house three months:

And when he was cast out, Pharaoh's daughter took him up, and nourished him for her own son.

And Moses was learned in all the wisdom of the Egyptians, and was mighty in words and in deeds.

And when he was full forty years old, it came into his heart to visit his brethren the children of Israel.

And seeing one of them suffer wrong, he defended him, and avenged him that was oppressed, and smote the Egyptian:

For he supposed his brethren would have understood how that God by his hand would deliver them: but they understood not.

And the next day he shewed himself unto them as they strove, and would have set them at one again, saying, Sirs, ye are brethren; why do ye wrong one to another?

But he that did his neighbour wrong thrust him away, saying, Who made thee a ruler and a judge over us?

Wilt thou kill me, as thou diddest the Egyptian yesterday?

Then fled Moses at this saying, and was a stranger in the land of Madian, where he begat two sons.

And when forty years were expired, there appeared to him in the wilderness of mount Sina an angel of the Lord in a flame of fire in a bush.

When Moses saw it, he wondered at the sight: and as he drew near to behold it, the voice of the Lord came unto him,

Saying, I am the God of thy fathers, the God of Abraham, and the God of Isaac, and the God of Jacob. Then Moses trembled, and durst not behold.

Then said the Lord to him, Put off thy shoes from thy feet: for the place where thou standest is holy ground.

I have seen, I have seen the affliction of my people which is in Egypt, and I have heard their groaning, and am come down to deliver them. And now come, I will send thee into Egypt.

This Moses whom they refused, saying, Who made thee a ruler and a judge? the same did God send to be a ruler and a deliverer by the hand of the angel which appeared to him in the bush.

He brought them out, after that he had shewed wonders and signs in the land of Egypt, and in the Red sea, and in the wilderness forty years.

This is that Moses, which said unto the children of Israel, A prophet shall the Lord your God raise up unto you of your brethren, like unto me; him shall ye hear.

Do you feel rejected by your friends? You are losing the shoes. Here lately it seems like doors are being slammed in my face. I shared in my last book how I prayed to have what Kathryn Kuhlman had. The other day I really felt rejected. God spoke to me and said "Don't you think Kathryn felt the same way you do?" Ouch! I have to lose the shoes. I cannot go into the next level in the same shoes. Why? Because I have outgrown them.

This is he, that was in the church in the wilderness with the angel which spake to him in the mount Sina, and with our fathers: who received the lively oracles to give unto us:

To whom our fathers would not obey, but thrust him from them, and in their hearts turned back again into Egypt,

Saying unto Aaron, Make us gods to go before us: for as for this Moses, which brought us out of the land of Egypt, we wot not what is become of him.

And they made a calf in those days, and offered sacrifice unto the idol, and rejoiced in the works of their own hands.

Then God turned, and gave them up to worship the host of heaven; as it is written in the book of the prophets, O ye house of Israel, have ye offered to me slain beasts and sacrifices by the space of forty years in the wilderness? Acts 7:20-42.

Picture this scene. Moses had feld from Egypt. He went to the backside of the desert and was tending sheep. Suddenly he notices a bush was on fire. When he turned to see the sight he heard a voice. What would you do? I was called up for prayer one Sunday morning. I was running from God at the time. As I was being prayed for I dropped to my knees. Suddenly the Holy Ghost spoke through me "Behold the burning bush." God wants to talk to us in the midst of our burning bush. We may be in the back side of the desert. It may be dry and dusty. Take heart because there is a burning bush. That burning bush contains our deliverance. Your life will not be the same when you behold the burning bush.

God told Moses to take his shoes off because he was on holy ground. Moses had to shed his wineskin in order to take on the wineskin God wanted him to have. *Rend your hearts not your garments* Joel 2:13. We must be willing to take spiritual inventory of our lives. That is not an easy task. Sometimes it can be painful.

Moses could never stand on holy ground in dirty sandals. He had to remove them. You and I can not stand where God wants us in the garments we have on now. We must change them. Looking back at Joseph in comparison to this scene, Jospeh shaved and changed his clothes before he went to stand before the king. He did not stand before him in prison garments. He had to completely change. Moses had to lose the shoes. We must loose the shoes in order to receive the proper footwear for the assignment before us.

What happens when we outgrow a pair of shoes? Our feet begin to hurt. Our toes are scrunched up inside the shoes. That is the same way spiritually. God is dealing with me as I am typing this. When we move into a new level, the clothes we had on in the last level shrink. They are the same size because that never changes. We have changed by growing, and the clothes no longer fit us. Yet we still want to come into this level with our same shoes on. Well these shoes are my favorite shoes and I don't want to part with them. Grandma did it this way for years and I don't want to change it now.

We wonder why we are crabby and nothing is going right. Come on now, I'm at this point. God is telling us to lose the shoes and we are still trying to keep them on our feet. Moses had to take off his shoes and to get to the level we are going in God we do too.

When God called Moses he began to make excuses. After he saw the burning bush. After he heard the voice of God calling him from the burning bush, he still made excuses. He said he could not speak well. God had a remedy for that. He chose Aaron to be the mouth piece for Moses. When God wants us to do something, don't we think God has a backup plan?

All Moses had to do was use the rod that was in his hand and Aaron would do the talking. It is amazing how God thinks. He truly thinks of everything. God had Moses in mind for this task long before now. He had this plan for Moses before Moses was born.

For I know the thoughts I think toward you, saith the Lord. Thoughs of peace and not of evil; to give you an expected end Jeremiah 29:11.

God knew Moses was going to make excuses that is why he chose Aaron to go with him. God knows our strenghs and he knows our limitations. We do not need to tell him we are not qualified. He already knows without him we are not qualified. Read this scripture.

Moreover whom he did predestinate, them he also called: and whom he called, them he also justified: and whom he justified, them he also glorified. Romans 8:30. God qualified Moses. Moses did not have to toot his horn because moses knew on his own he wasn't qualified. Only through the grace of God was Moses going to do what he was called to do. You and I are in the same situation.

We can't do anything on our own because we will mess it up. Thanks to the fall, aside from God, even our best is our worst. We cannot do anything unless he enables us. *I can do all things through Christ, which strengthens me* Phillipians 4:13. When we come to realize that truth our lives will change forever. *In him we live and move and have our being* Acts 17:28. What joy it is to know he is our source. He takes the impossible in us and turns it into the possible. Hallelujah!!

Chapter 3

Exodus: From Slavery to Deliverance as by Blood

The book of Exodus blesses me because although the children of Israel was in slavery, God sends a deliverer, this man named Moses. God always has a plan and purpose for things that take place in our lives. We may not always see it, but, *All things work together for the good to those that love him; and are the called according to his purpose* Romans 8:28.

God was very meticulous when he gave Moses his assignment. He took Moses' limitations and turned them into strengths. That is how he is with us.

Pharoah was a slave master. In my view, his reign could be compared to the reign of Hitler's reign in Germany. Hitler hated the Jews to the point of having them killed. Pharoah was scared of the Jews. He was scared so much he made slaves out of them.

Moses was sent as the deliverer because of the covenant God made with Jacob. He promised Jacob they would enter Egypt, but he would bring them back into their own land again. *God is not a God that he should lie; nor the son of man that he should repent; hath he said and shall he not do it? Or hath he spoken, and shall he not make it good?* Numbers 23:19.

Through the limitations of Moses God used what was in Hoses' hand to perform miracles. God used a rod. Why a rod? Moses was tending sheep in the desert. A shepherd has to use a rod to not only corral the sheep, but (watch this) to protect them.

The Lord is my shepherd, I lack nothing.

He makes me lie down in green pastures,

he leads me beside quiet waters,

he refreshes my soul. He guides me along the right paths for his name's sake.

Even though I walk through the darkest valley, I will fear no evil, for you are with me, your **rod and your staff,** *they comforet me.*

You prepare a table before me in the presence of my enemies,. You anoint my head with oil; my cup overflows.

Surely your goodness and love will follow me, will follow me all the days of my life, and I will dwell in the house of the Lord forever Psalm 23. Notice I used a boldface on rod and your staff. I did this to show the similarities between Moses and the shepherd of our souls Jesus.

A couple of things happen according to the twenty third Psalm when the rod and staff comforts us.

1. God prepares a table before us in the presences of our enemies. Because Jesus is the shepherd even our enemies have no choice but to be at peace with us. I prophesy to you right now that some of your biggest support will come from your enemies. Don't think it cannot happen because it can. When my car needs fixed, I don't pay for it, those that hate me do. That is

true. I can share stories with you on how this happens. God is going to give you so much favor with your enemies that they are going to pay for things not knowing why they are doing it. Instead of being your greatest hinderance, I declare they are going to be your greatest supporter.

2. You anoint my head with oil. I declare a fresh anointing over your life. God enjoys anointing his people. Those the world think is useless God anoints and makes useful. David was just a shepherd until Samuel anointed him as the next king. You do not know what is inside you until the anointing comes. You feel worthless because everything you touch seems to fail. When the anointing comes, God takes your failure and makes it a success. Who am I talking to? After Samuel anointed David king he didn't immediately contend for the the throne. He went back to the field and tended sheep. I'm going to say this in love because I used to be this way. Some get anointed by God in a church service and they expect to immediately be allowed a pass to the front of the line. Let me explain. At sixteen or seventeen-years-old God called me to preach. I preached at home to my teddy bears all the time. When I accepted the calling I was so excited that I went and told my pastor Brother Utley. To my amazement we didn't go straight to the pulpit. We went outside and around to the back of the church. He opened up the door and showed me the lawn mower. My new job was to mow the yard. My mom was the secretary of the church, and she made sure I mowed

the yard. I was so mad at him for that. I thought he did not recognize my calling, but he did. If we can't tend to the job God puts in front of us how can we tend to our calling? He allowed me to preach my first message. I shared this in my last book. I preached on Put God First. I had it all written out word for word. Remember I could preach for hours to my teddy bears, but they are not living and breathing things. I read that message word for word and it took all of five minutes. No sweat poured off me. No hallelujahs came out of my mouth. Nothing, just reading words. I went to Brother Utley and told him I was done and that I was a failure. He told me something I will never forget. He said, "Tracy you can't quit. Get on your bicycle and ride again." David went back to the field. In the time of being in the field, he wrote some of the greatest Psalms such as Psalm 23. When God was ready for him to take the throne he took it. God has a timetable for you. When he is ready for you to shine Hell cannot cause you to become dull

3. Your cup will run over. The song says; When I think of the goodness of Jesus; and all he has done for me. My soul cries out hallelujah. Praise God for saving me. The great shepherd will bring you joy. The Holy Ghost will come upon you and when he comes (not it), he does not come alone. He comes bringing joy unspeakable and full of glory. Are you ready for this joy?

Here is some scriptures on correction from the Lord and how we are suppose to deal with it.

Behold, happy is the man whom God correcteth: therefore despise not thou the chastening of the Almighty: Job 5:17

My son, despise not the chastening of the LORD; neither be weary of his correction:

For whom the LORD loveth he correcteth; even as a father the son in whom he delighteth. Proverbs 3:11-12.

And ye have forgotten the exhortation which speaketh unto you as unto children, My son, despise not thou the chastening of the Lord, nor faint when thou art rebuked of him:

For whom the Lord loveth he chasteneth, and scourgeth every son whom he receiveth.

If ye endure chastening, God dealeth with you as with sons; for what son is he whom the father chasteneth not?

But if ye be without chastisement, whereof all are partakers, then are ye bastards, and not sons.

Furthermore we have had fathers of our flesh which corrected us, and we gave them reverence: shall we not much rather be in subjection unto the Father of spirits, and live?

For they verily for a few days chastened us after their own pleasure; but he for our profit, that we might be partakers of his holiness.

Now no chastening for the present seemeth to be joyous, but grievous: nevertheless afterward it yieldeth the peaceable fruit of righteousness unto them which are exercised thereby.

Wherefore lift up the hands which hang down, and the feeble knees;

And make straight paths for your feet, lest that which is lame be turned out of the way; but let it rather be healed. Hebews 12:5-13.

It is not fun getting disciplined from the Lord but it is needful. His rod of correction brings life. I want to say something that many may not agree with. Parents we are responsible for our children. When we withhold correction it is us not them that are being held accountable. Let me also say, states that ban using the rod of correction is going to face judgment. I'm not saying beat the child, but a swat on the rear does not harm a child. God will judge those that spare the rod. I'm sorry for being so blunt, but the word of God plainly tells us how to discipline our children. The government has stepped in and taken the rights away from the parents and given it to the children. God will judge this behavior. Why do we see school shootings today? The children are in control. When I was growing up we did not back talk our parents. Today, it is expected if not praised. Well the kids have a voice some might say. Yes they have a voice because the world has given it to them. God wants the children to obey the parents and not the parents obey the children. Come on now. If America does not repent at the burning bush for allowing the children to take over the home, America will see destruction. You cannot go against God's order and survive.

When Moses used the rod, Aaron did not go behind him and tell him not to use it. Aaron spoke to Pharoah and Moses used the rod of judgment and correction. It is time order be restored back into the home.

With the rod, he turned water into blood. He stretched the rod out and there was a plague of frogs, lice, locust, and darkness. Even with all those marvel powers Pharoah did like we do today, he hardened his heart.

God told Moses in Exodus 12 to have the people kill a lamb. Take the blood of the lamb and put it on the doorpost and lentils of their house (signifying the heart). God told Moses the death angel was going to pass through that night. He promised, "When I see the blood I will pass over you." Isn't that wonderful? God isn't looking for talents. He isn't looking for gifts. He is looking for the blood. What can wash away my sins? Nothing but the blood of Jesus. What can make me whole again? Nothing but the blood of Jesus. Oh precious is the flow. That makes me whilte as snow. No other fount I know. Nothing but the blood of Jesus.

What is the significance of the blood? Wikipedia says; In the Torah, the blood of this sacrifice painted on the door- posts of the Israelites was to be a sign to God, when passing through the land to slay the firstborn of the Egyptians, that he should pass by the houses of the Israelites. In the Mishnah it is called the "Passover of Egypt." It should be repeated annually." God thought this event was so important that it should be celebrated annually. In a sense, this celebration is erectinga stone of remembrance. We are saying look what the Lord has done.

As we accept Jesus into our life, the blood is applied to the doorpost of our heart. This causes us to be in right standing with him. Our sins are no longer seen because the blood of Jesus becomes ourr passover. Glory!!

The Preacher's Word tells about a story of a Jewish father telling his son about the events of the passover. He tells in detail the account of what happened when the events of the passover took place. As the author stated, the story he was telling the boy was different because of the resemblance of the passover to the Messiah. "There was the slaying of a flawless lamb, the passover feast. Eating unleavened bread. Roasting the meat and preparing it with bitter herbs. Smearing the blood on the doorpost, which spared the lives of their firstborn {sic}. This year the story is different. It takes on a new meaning. A prophetic fulfillment. Jesus of Nazareth, who was hailed as the lamb of God has been crucified before the passover (Preacher's Word).

I believe when the death angel passed over the land that night and saw the blood on the door, he saw the blood of Jesus. I've been taught the Word of God is about types and shadows. On the day of the crucifixion Jesus became the lamb. When they whipped him and the blood flowed, that blood fleshed out the symbolism of the blood the children of Israel put on the doorpost. To go further back into history, he became the ram caught in the thicket for Abraham.

When we accept Jesus death has to pass over. The blood of Jesus is so pure and powerful that our sins are not only covered but washed away with just one drop. Maxwell House coffee says it is good to the last drop. The blood of Jesus is good to the initial drop.

Jesus doesn't see all the times we mess up. He doesn't remember how we rebelled against his word. When the father sees the blood of the spotless Paschal lamb we go from his judgment to redemption. I can picture that Jewish father sitting his son down and telling hm the story. The son's face lights up as he sits listening intently to every word. He has the expression on his face that tells his father "DadI got it." I believe that is how Heaven reacts to us. The father has joy in his heart because the son understands the story of the passover. Our heavenly father has joy in his heart when we accept the sacrifice he in the role of Abraham has given us in the role of Issaac. The celebration doesn't start and end with the father. *Likewise, I say unto you, there is joy in the presence of the angels of God over one sinner that repents* Luke 15:10. In Luke 15 Jesus is giving the parable of a woman that lost a coin. She swept the house and finally found the coin she lost. When she found it she was so excited she called people over for a celebration. That is how salvation is treated by God. There is a celebration in Heaven when the blood of the Paschal lamb is applied to the door-post and lintil of someone's heart. The sinner goes from being cast out to being grafted in. Suddenly, the sin that drove the sinner out of his or her garden of Eden is forgiven and that person is then grafted into the vine of the father because of the blood of Jesus. Hallelujah!!

Have you been to Jesus for your cleansing? I'm not asking you if you shook the preacher's hand. Have you accepted the sacrifice Jesus gave you? I'm going to close this chapter with the chorus of a song.

It reaches to the highest mountain. It flows from the lowest valley. The blood that gives me strength from day to day. It will never lose its power.

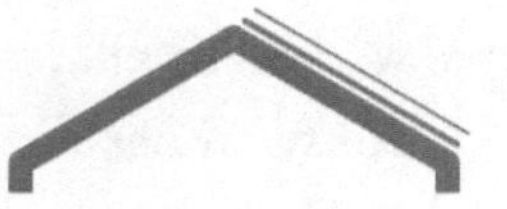

Chapter 4
BEHOLD THE LAMB

Now behold the lamb. The precious lamb of God. Born into sin so I could live again. The precious lamb of God. What a wonderful worship song. This lamb was gentle. He was pure and divine. This lamb was the son of God. He left the splendors of Heaven to come to earth. When he was to be born there was no where he was accepted. All the places were full. (Like we are today). His mother found the only place she could, a stable. We are that stable. I feel the Holy Ghost. Sin caused the inns to be full. Some inns are full of pride. Some inns are full of hatred, but all are full. The only place that accepts the precious gift of the Paschal lamb is the stable. Why? Because the stable is a place where you can abandon all. It is a place no one wants to be in. Seperation from the world is no problem when you are in the stable. Pride can't touch you in a lonely smelly stable. This is the perfect place to birth this precious gift. I wonder how Mary and Joseph felt when they were turned away from places. She was ready to give birth but no where to do it. We are ready to give birth to something in the spirit. Wher are we going to find a place to birth what is inside us? You guessed it, the stable.

Even at birth people wanted to kill Jesus. King Herod wanted to kill him out of jealousy. What did he do? He did what Pharoah did in Moses' day. He ordered all the males children to be killed. Can you see the similarity between Moses and Jesus? Just as God rescued Moses he rescued Jesus.

Moses was driven to the backside of the desert to receive his ministry. After Jesus was baptized by john the Baptist, he was driven to a mountain to fast for forty days and nights. Moses argued with and lost at the burning bush. Jesus argued and won against Satan on the mountain. Many similarities between the two deliverors because they are in the same lineage.

There are other accounts in the bible where there was recognition of the lamb. Bible Truths has an article titled Jesus Christ is the Passover Lamb. They listed 101 bible verses that prove Jesus is the passover lamb. While I am not going to list all, of them, I am going to mention those that caught my eye. We are going to look at Cain and Abel first. "We aren't told how Cain and Abel knew God required a blood sacrifice, but we know they did because God rebuked Cain for not doing what he knew to do. In many ways this is the real first passover in the bible. Genesis 4:3-7, Hebrew 11:4 (Bible Truths).

In this account we get the understanding how powerful blood is. Cain got jealous because Abel's offering was accepted and his wasn't. Cain did not offer a sufficient sacrifice. He offered from the crops which represents the natural. Abel offered a blood sacrifice representing the spirtitual. Romans 12:1 gives us insight on why God accepted Abel's sacrifice. Let's look at it:

*I bessech you therefore, brethern, by the mercies of God, that ye present your bodies a **living sacrifice, holy, acceptable unto God, which is your reasonable service*** (KJV). Notice the bold sentence. God wanted a sacrifice that came from the heart. A living sacrifice. Abel had the right heart. How did he know what type of sacrifice to offer? When your heart is right discernment kicks in. Is it possible thousands of years before The Sacrifice came into the world that there was going to be a blood sacrifice given for the world? We do not know because scripture does not say. We do know however, Abel offered the right sacrifice and Cain did not. Jealousy killed Abel.

The bible tells us when God spoke to Cain and asked where Abel was that Cain told God he was not his brother's keeper. God told him Abel's blood cries from the ground. Now that is powerful. Blood speaks. Foreinsics will tell you that DNA speaks. Where is the main thing they extract DNA from? Blood. The DNA evidence convicted Cain of Abel's murder.

I watch a lot of Invesitgative Discovery. It is fascinating how they can pin point a killer. If there is a struggle, (and in order for Cain to kill Abel there almost had to be one), the killer's blood gets on the victim. They can take that blood and match it to the guilty party by way of DNA. There are other ways DNA is matched but this is not Criminal Justice class.

When God told Cain Abel's blood is crying from the ground he basicaly told him you are busted. Friend it takes the blood to be accepted by God. Without the blood we have the spirit of Cain. We can shout and run the aisle in church looking all spiritual and be filled with the spirit of Cain. Cain walked and talked with Abel. They were brothers. One thing that seperated the two was the administration of spirits. Abel had the spirit of God and Cain had the spirit of flesh. It showed in the sacrifice they made.

You can say what you want but Abel was the first one that prophesied about the blood of Jesus. Long before the children of Israel had to put the blood on the doorpost signifying Passover, Abel prophesied there would be a blood sacrifice. Hebrews says this: *to Jesus the mediator of a new covenant, and to the sprinkled blood that speaks a better word than the blood of Abel* Hebrews 12:24.Somehow the actions of Abel whether he realized it or not paved the way for the atoning work of the blood of Jesus. Abel's sacrifice became the type and shadow of the blood of Christ. That blood, Jesus' blood speakes louder than Abel's ever could. Jesus' blood does more than Abel's did. Abel's blood went to the grave with him and ceased. Jesus' blood went from the whipping post to Calvary. From Calvary it followed him to the grave. While in the grave, the blood followed Jesus to Hell and loosed the captives. From Hell the blood of Jesus rose with him from the grave and ascended back with Jesus to Heaven. Finally, from there his blood washes away the sins of those that accept the plan of salvation. What a conversation the blood of Jesus makes.

Let's look at some ways blood speaks to us. When a baby is born blood speaks to who the father is. Again, DNA is extracted through the blood. When a praternity test is done they use the blood from the father and the baby to help determine.

Blood speaks letting us know when we are sick. They can do blood tests to determine the type of sickness you have. For diabetics the blood determines the blood sugar level in the blood stream. They run blood tests to determine if a person has HIV. So we see blood speaks in the medical field.

Blood speaks in the Criminal Justice field as well. As we have already discussed they can use DNA sometimes in the saliva but also through the blood to determine a suspect. They can use blood to help idieentify a person if the person is unidentifiable. Mabny other ways blood can be used in the criminal justice field. Blood spatter at a crime scene tells a major story to the investigators.

They use blood to determine blood type. If a person needs a blood transfusion they must find the right blood type. The person wanting to give blood must take a blood test to find out if their blood is compatible. This procedure is also done when a person is donating an organ.

Now we can see why when Cain killed Abel how there was so much power in the blood. One of my favorite songs is there is power, power, wonder working power. In the blood of the lamb. There is power, power, wonder working power. In the precious blood of the lamb. We will look more into the power of the blood in the next chapter.

In another online article titled What is the Passover Lamb, How Jesus is our Passover Lamb, the author states; "Jesus is our passover lamb. He was slaughtered so we might be saved. His blood is the sacrifice that covered the penalty of our sins once and for all" (Compelling Truth). I remember watching the movie the Passion of the Christ. Although this was a silent picture sound would have done it injustice. The scenes of the horrible beating he suffered. As they were beating him we get a glimpse of a man walking by wearing all black laughing. This man signified Satan. You could not help watching with tears as they beat him. He looked like hamburger when they were done with him. Through all the beating he never opened his mouth. He could have called legions of angels to stop the horrific beating, but he didn't.

He was wounded for our transgressions. He was bruised for our iniquities. Surely he bore our sorrows. And by his stripes we are healed. Do we really know what we are singing? To some these words are just another song. To me they are the reason I exist. What are they to you?

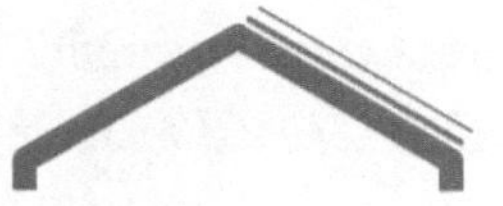

Chapter 5

SONGS ABOUT THE BLOOD

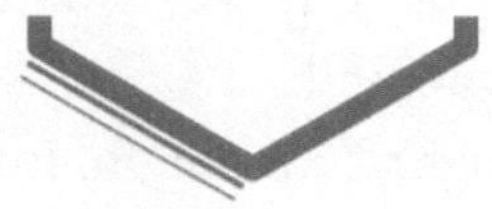

I remember as a kid sitting in church singing songs about the blood. The spirit began to move. Suddenly a sister would start shouting and running the aisle. All Brother Utley could do was lift his hands and say hallelujah. Why did the spirit move when we sang about the blood?

Today the same songs are in the hymn books but we have outgrew the song books. It I sad to say the blood has lost its impact on the church today. We no longer get excited about the blood like they did in the old days. Now we want other songs to fill our Sunday morning worship service. What happened to the blood?

In this short chapter I am going to share some of the songs I grew up with that talks about the blood. While these songs will not win a popularity contest today the message is more real than ever. In my Facebook livesI still sing the older songs about the blood, and why wouldn't I? If it wasn't for the blood we would be lost. If it wasn't for the blood we would not be healed. The blood of Jesus is more powerful than any remedy they come up with today. More potent than a COVID vaccine. The blood has been tested and passed with flying colors. The FDA does not need to put the stamp of approval on the blood because God already approved it for centuries to come.

There is power, power, wonder working power; in the blood of the lamb. There is power, power, wonder working power. In the precious blood of the lamb.

It reaches to the highest mountain. It flows from the lowest valley. The blood that gives me strngth from day to day. Will never lose its power.

Are you washed in the blood? In the soul cleansing blood of the lamb. Are your garments spotless are they white as snow? Are you washed in the blood of the lamb? One of the verses says; Lay aside the garments that are stained with sin, and be washed in the blood of the lamb. Ther's a fountain flowing for the soul unclean. Oh be washed in the blood of the lamb.

As we sang songs like this we would sing like we really meant it. I want to see people get excited while they sing about the blood of Jesus. If there was no calvary there would be no redemption. Without redemption we would be in Hell. Isn't the blood worth singing about? I think so.

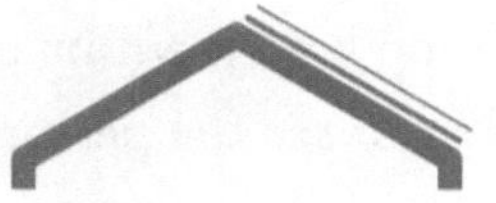

Chapter 6
From the doorpost to the Cross

One of the most fascinating stories is when the children of Israel demonstrated Passover. Moses had used the rod to show Pharoah how powerful God was. He stretched out the rod and nine plagues came upon the earth. Pharoah's heart was hardened because his magicians could do some of them. Can I interject her and tell you Satan is a con- artist and can imitate God.

Satan appears as an angel of light; *And no wonder, for **Satan himself masquerades as an angel of light**. It is not surprising, then, if his servants also masquerade as servants of righteousness. Their end will be what their actions deserve* 2 Corinthians 11:14-15.

Can I tell you, Satan can run the aisle and shout in the house of God. He is good at it. Sometimes Satan can go undetected in a church service because of the lack of discernment. I have personally seen this. The person can sit in the service and pretend to be holy until the spirit begins to move in a greater manner. As you begin to watch this person they begin to get uncomfortable. Satan cannot stand under the true power of God. He flees when he is around the true power of God.

We as children of God have it wrong many times when dealing with this. We expect to see the person possessed to foam at the mouth and move around like a snake because Hollywood portrays that. That does happen sometimes but many times it does not. Let me share an experience with you. I was praying for a lady in Herrin Illinois. The Holy Ghost showed me she was having dreams of a dark figure with a sickle. The grim reaper. I spoke this out and under her breath she told me "I am going to kill you." I rebuked the devil and he left her. She did not throw herself on the ground and hiss. She stood there in the prayer line pretending to be holy. That is what Moses was up against. The magicians were a type and shadow of Satan in 2 Corinthians 11: 14-15. He could do what Moses did because Satan knew the true power of God. He spent time with God in Heaven. He spends time with God in the Court of Heaven as well.

There is a saying that fits here, often imitated but never duplicated. Satan can imitate God but he can never duplicate him. There were some things God did through Moses the magicians could try to imitate but the results were not duplicated. God tore Egypt up. Egypt was Satan's territory. There is a song that says, We're going up to the high places to tear Satan's kingdom down. Moses had to go up high in order to thwart Satan's plans.

When we learn we must go higher than we are now we will see greater victories. Satan did not care that Moses had a rod. He did not care how much he stretched the rod out. He only cared when the magicians couldn't duplicate some of the wonders. As long as you don't get too close to God you do not become a target. The minute you begin to seek after the things of God, Satan will target you. He will target you and your family with everything he has.

My family moved from Fort Wayne indiana to Mount Vernon Illinois in 2019. As long as we were talking about the move we were fine. The moment the u- haul was loaded and we were on our way Satan's plan was in effect. We stayed with my oldest son from December 2019 to February 2020. Once we found a place to live we became a target. As long as the magicians could immitate the miracles Moses was fine. Pharoah's heart stayed hard and he could play mind games with Moses. Once God raised the stakes and exposed the magicians for frauds Moses became a target. Pharoah threatened to kill Moses if he ever showed his face around there again. Why? Satan could immitate but never duplicate.

Each time Pharoah refused to let the Children of Israel go God raised the stakes. We must remember the promise God made not only Abraham,but Jacob as well. Before Jacob was born Abraham whose name was Abram got a taste of Egypt. Abram lied telling Pharoah Sari was his sister. One mistake could have cost Pharoah his life, but God preserved him. God promised Abram now called Abraham he would cause him to prosper and be a possessor of the land. Satan knew and understood this.

Years later Jacob now being called Israel was a full fledge citizen of Egypt. Remember I told you Joseph had a dream that his brothers and father would bow to him. Not only did they bow to him, but he caused them to get land in Goshen which could be like a suburb of Egypt. I wonder what went through Satan's mind as God's chosen people were in Egypt?

After Joseph died the Pharoah that was over Egypt died as well. Another Pharoah took over that did not know of God. There is always someone standing in the wing waiting for their turn. The Anti-christ is waiting to make the grand appearance on this earth just as the evil Pharoah did upon Egypt. We need to be sober at all times.

God called a moses to deliver Israel because of the promise he made to Jacob. He told Jacob he was going down to Egypt and that he would bring him back again. What has God promised you? God will always I repeat always keep his word.

With a rod in his hand and the authority of God Moses did gret wonders in Egypt, but it never phased Pharoah. God knew he had to raise the stakes one last time. He had Moses tell the people to kill a lamb. They were suppose to take the blood of the lamb and put it on the doorpost and lentils of their house. The death angel was going to pass through Egypt and kill the first-born of Egypt. The blood was a token to Israel that the angel would pass over them. The blood of Jesus applied to your life will cause judgment to pass over your life. Sickness and disease cannot overtake you while you are under the influence of the blood of Jesus.

That night the angel passed over Israel as promised but killed the first born in Egypt. This is amazing to me. The original covenant was between Abraham and God. God asked Abraham to take his only son (not the firstborn of the flesh but of the spirit) which was Jacob's dad Isaac, and offer him as a sacrifice. Because of Abraham's obedience Isaac was spared. Now some hundreds of years later because of sin and disobedience Pharoah caused all olf Egypt, including himself to lose their firstborn.

The blood saved Israel. The blood can save you. A couple weeks ago I weasd at work getting ready to clock in. A prophet from Africa whom I have never met got in contact with me. He began to prophesy over me how there was no peace in my home. He was right because my home got split apart almost 3 years ago. It has been my wife and I. Can I tell you it has been Hell. I have to battle depression, not only for my wife's soul, but to try to keep it from overtaking me. I am tired.

He began to tell me there was people in my own family that was my enemy. They hated me and was working against me. God showed me this two years ago, but I kept it to myself. He began to pray witchcraft off of me and my family. He said, "Your family is suppose to move but witchcraft is preventing it." A frsh fight rose up in me. He told me to watch what God does.

Thursday of that week we foud out my daughter was coming home on Christmas break. Can I tell you when the blood is applied to your life witchcraft can try to work, but it cannot win out. Like the magicians, witchcraft can immitate but cannot duplicate what God is doing in your life. Hallelujah!!

Hundreds of years after Israel came out of Egypt the paschal lamb was born. I touched on it two chapters back. There was physically no room in the popular places so this lamb was born in an unpopular place, the stable. Quit trying to fit in. You will never fit into the world's design again. The bible says, *Therefore, Come out from them and be seperate, says the Lord. Touch no unclean thing, and I will receive you.*

And, I will be a father to you, and you will be my sons and daughters, says the Lord almighty 2 Corinthians 6:17-18.

Why didn't Jesus fit in? He was not of this world. Did you catch that? He was from above. He was apart of creation. His blood was symbollically on the doorpost and lentils of the houses of Israel. He would never fit in.

As a believer you do not fit in either. You can try to fit in, but you will stick out like a sore thumb. I have never been able to fit in anywhere. I was hated at school. I showed up and was instantly picked on. Even the new kids picked on me. How did they know to pick on me? I didn't wear an outward sign telling them to pick on me. I found out because of my destiny I carried an inward sign that told people I was an alien in this life.

My friends were Batman, Superman and the Lone Ranger. I imagined I could fly. When I tell you I imagined I could fly, I literally saw myself flying. I got in a swing going as high as I could go. As my swing swung upward, I jumped out saying up, up, and away. I pictured myself flying like Superman. I was nine years old at the time.

I never realized the symbolism between myself picturing myself flying and this scripture in Isaiah; *But those that hope in the Lord will renew their strength. They will soar on wings like eagles, they will run and not grow weary, they will walk and not be faint* Isaiah 40:31. Last year for my birthday my son got me an eagle statute with that verse on it. He did not know I liked that scripture.

While kids were outside playing on their bikes I was in my bedroom preaching to my teddy bears. What was wrong with me? I was different. When I did play outside I had to be the leader. If my sister, my niece and nephew played club I had to be the president. God was preparing me to be youth leader.

I shared these intimate details to give you a glimpse into the way the paschal lamb Jesus did not fit in. There are Christians that are about to give birth in the spirit that get offended when the in- crowd doesn't make room for them. "Sister Sally doesn't appreciate my gift. She doesn't know who I am." Come on now we have all been there. What happened? There was no room in sister Sally's inn to receive you. She didn't mean anything by it, and may not realize she slighted you. Her level does not match what is taking place inside your spirit.

The inns were not ready to receive Jesus. Even in the stable, Herod tried to kill him. The world wants to kill you even when things are going right. Why? Because we are not of this world. Pastor quit letting the congregation dictate whether you have peace or not. Your hope is in Jesus and not in man.

Not everyone that hangs around you is going to be an honored guest in your victory party. There are some people that are in your life by seasons. This season they are with you but next season you notice they got offended and walk away. As long as you live close to them they are there. The minute God moves you somewhere else you are forgotten. We went through this in Fort Wayne Indiana. The church we went through supported us while we lived in Indiana. We moved to Illinois, and when the storm hit, they abandoned us. They were in this season for a reason.

As Jesus was walking the earth and doing miracles the disciples were with him. This was their season. They learned a lot from the master in this season. They watched him do miracles, turn the water into wine, and walk on the water. They were sitting under the learning tree of the paschal lamb.

As time drew closer for the ram to be caught in the thicket the disciples turned from him in time of need. Peter received a name change. He received the keys to the kingdom. When it came time to acknowledge Jesus during the master's time of need, he abandoned him. Why? Different season.

You're in this season for a reason. You may not see the reasoning now. We recently lost my nephew. Although we are all devastated by the loss, his life is touching more people now than he ever did while he was here. You are in preparation for the next season. There may be moments of severe pain and hurts now. You may be laying on your pillow at night crying yourself to sleep. You are carrying your next season. I feel the Holy Ghost.

I prophesy you are searching for a place to give birth. Don't look at the high and lofty places. Your baby is not meant for luxury. In the manger you will find rest. Oooo. You won't find victory at the bank of the Jordan river. You will find solace in Gethsemane. That is the place you lay your will down and pick up his will. The blood of the paschal lamb will meet you in that lonely garden and wash you clean. Even at the whipping post, standing all alone, Jesus remained steadfast to the mission. Are you steadfast the call?

Mike bowling wrote a song the Call. It says; Remind me Lord you called me. Sometimes I may get weary. If a soul has been saved it's worth it all. When I see those teardorps falling. Remind me of my callimg May I never run from the call.

Jesus went to the cross in order for you to receive your calling. He is calling you now to himself. You won;t find him at the Marriot. You will find him in the stable. He is not going to be hanging around the dignitaries. He is in Gethsemane. He won't be lying in a nice elegant casket but will be on a cross. The paschal lamb is searching far and wide. When he sees the blood he will pass over you.

Conclusion

As I sat in my Sunday School class, I did not realize the magnitude of the teaching I received. Sunday School was a ritual to me. The sad fact is, I did not know the beauty of what Jesus did for me. I was blessed to be forgiven and didn't realize it. You have the same opportunity to be forgiven.

Jesus is calling you. He wants you to take the blood from the paschal lamb and apply it to the doorpost of your heart. All you have to do is pray and ask God into your heart. I invite you to pray this prayer.

Father I have sinned against Heaven and you. I deserve the death angel to visit my house, but I ask you to forgive me. Lord I want to take the blood of the paschal lamb and apply it to the doorpost of my heart. Wash mne and cleanse me. Take me to Gethsemane that I may learn your will. In Yeshua's name, Amen.

DEDICATION

I would like to dedicate this book to the memory of my Sunday School teacher Sister Hester. She spent tireless Sundays teaching me the truth. She never complained when I stood up laying hands on everyone in my class and pray for them.

I was a hellion but she was patient. We need more teachers like her. Those that teach the word the way it is suppose to be. I honor you Sister Hester and will see you again.

Special Thanks

I want to thank the pascal lamb for giving the ultimate sacrifice. He gave his life for us. I want to thank my spiritual father Apostle David E. Taylor for holding my family up in prayer. We would not be where we are without your teaching. I am so thankful your staff introduced mne to your ministry.

<u>Http://www.joshuamediaministies.org</u>[1]

---

1.   http://www.joshuamediaministies.org/

Contact us

We would love to minister in your church or come and do a book signing. You can contact us at:

greaterdeliveranceministries7@gmail.com

(618) 315-3330

cash app:$greaterdeliverance15

Don't miss out!

Visit the website below and you can sign up to receive emails whenever Tracy Henderson publishes a new book. There's no charge and no obligation.

https://books2read.com/r/B-A-XBQU-CUFCC

BOOKS2READ

Connecting independent readers to independent writers.

Also by Tracy Henderson

Inheritance Series
Inheritance by Fire

Standalone
Gabbi's Amazing Dream
`When I See the Blood

About the Author

As a child I was raised in church. I wasn't sent to church I was taken. I accepted my call to preach at seventeen years old, but something was missing. I had religion, but not relationship. In June of 2019 God gloriously saved me. It was an Apostle Paul like conversion. I was lying in bed on June 5, 2019 and developed chest pains and could not talk. Suddenly a bright light appeared to me, and I was taken out of my body. As I was taken up I heard the words "You have not delivered my message yet", and I was set back down. I was introduced to one of my spiritual fathers Apostle David E. Taylor in 2019, by a staff member. I wasn't quite sure he was for real until I had a vision about him and I in a hospital praying for people. He introduced me to spiritual inheritance through a book he wrote on it. Since then I have been on a quest to find the true meaning of spiritual inheritance. I pray not only through my ministry of preaching, but through my writing I am able to deliver God's message. I pray as people read my material their lives are changed as mine was. That will be my legacy I leave to the world.

www.ingramcontent.com/pod-product-compliance
Lightning Source LLC
Chambersburg PA
CBHW021759150726
47989CB00004B/1725